POPULAR
NURSERY
RHYMES

"In books, or works, or healthful play,
  Let my first years be past,
That I may give for every day
  Some good account at last". Watts

POPULAR
NURSERY
RHYMES

Edited by Jennifer Mulherin

Publishers
GROSSET & DUNLAP
New York

Editor
Jennifer Mulherin

Art Director
Tom Deas

Editorial and picture research
Patrick Rudd, Leila Kooros

ISBN: 0-448-01346-0.
Library of Congress Catalog Card No. 82-084693.

First published 1981 by Granada Publishing Limited.
Devised by Octavian Books Limited.
Copyright © Jennifer Mulherin 1981.

Published in the United States 1983 by Grosset & Dunlap, Inc.
Printed in Italy by New Interlitho, Milan.

CONTENTS

INTRODUCTION

A BOOK OF nursery rhymes must, first of all, delight children. The remarkable pictures in this book, many of which have rarely been seen before, will, one believes, do just that. If, together with these lilting rhymes, they stimulate the child's imagination, one has achieved no mean feat.

The illustrations are, in fact, a pictorial history of nursery rhyme illustration. The publishers of the earliest collections of nursery rhymes recognized, as we do today, that children above all love pictures. An illustration catches the attention of the childish mind far more than lines of print and even in the first books of nursery rhymes, each rhyme was accompanied by a little woodcut. Many of the illustrations reproduced here from Iona and Peter Opie's *The Oxford Nursery Rhyme Book* are taken from the chapbooks and toybooks of the early 18th and 19th centuries. Thomas Bewick and others executed these woodcuts which still have a remarkable charm and simplicity. The 19th century was the golden age of book illustration. Nothing has surpassed the stunningly beautiful coloured engravings of Walter Crane, Kate Greenaway and Randolph Caldecott, yet the hand-coloured engravings of the mid-19th century (interestingly, 'factory' produced), one of which accompanies 'Three little kittens, they lost their mittens' are surprisingly delightful. The illustrators of the early 20th century, whose work went into numerous reprints in the decades up to World War II, must surely evoke nostalgia. What reader does not recollect, in distant memory, the enchantment of Arthur Rackham's illustrations? These, with Charles Robinson's delicate line drawings, Charles Folkard's bold images and Leslie L. Brooke's soft melting colours have a remarkable and enduring appeal. There have, of course, been many very fine illustrators of nursery rhymes in the second half of this century, none of whom are included here. This is simply because one feels that these older pictures form a unity and have, above all, the undeniable quality of miniature works of art. No child or adult can surely resist their enchantment. It needs also to be pointed out that when historical personalities or events are associated with a rhyme efforts have been made to include an appropriate illustration. This not only adds interest but also an extra dimension to the rhymes and annotations.

In choosing these particular rhymes, one has selected the most popular. Almost all of these will be familiar, if not to the small child, at least to his parents. In many ways this is as much a book for adults as for children, for it is the former who are responsible for passing on these traditional rhymes and whose memories of childhood, half-forgotten lines of verse and childish experiences will be evoked by these delightful rhymes. It is doubtful if children are interested in the origins or significance of nursery rhymes – they enjoy the sounds, the rhythms, the repetitive chanting, and the simple tales or situations depicted – but for their parents these notes about historical personages and events, as well as the myths and rituals associated with the rhymes, may be of interest.

In compiling the notes to these rhymes, one has constantly borne in mind the words attributed to Hugo Grotius, the 17th century Dutch

jurist and scholar: 'It is a mean and scandalous practice in authors to put notes to things that deserve no notice'. Folklorists and scholars have written extensively about a great number of these rhymes, many of which are really inconsequential. They are simply lullabies, jingles, riddles and prayers passed on from generation to generation, often adapted and changed but, over the centuries, constantly repeated by children in the nursery, with or without the aid of the printed word. While drawing on the vast amount of literature written about these rhymes, the annotations have been kept to a minimum. Only what seems genuinely interesting and possibly accurate has been included. Readers interested in fuller studies of the origins and significance of nursery rhymes should look immediately to Iona and Peter Opie's authoritative work on the subject in *The Oxford Dictionary of Nursery Rhymes*. No writer on nursery rhymes today can do otherwise than acknowledge considerable indebtedness to this monumental work of scholarship. The pioneering work in the 19th century by James

This beautiful hand-coloured engraving for 'The cock crows in the morn' appears in John Harris's Little Rhymes for Little Folks *c1812. Harris was one of the best-known and most successful of the publishers of early children's books*

Orchard Halliwell ('one of the most indefatigable diggers in the history of scholarship') cannot go unmentioned, for it was he who, in *The Nursery Rhymes of England* (initially published in 1842) and *Popular Nursery Rhymes and Tales* (1849), first drew attention to the antiquity of nursery rhymes and made the first comprehensive collection of rhymes, on which almost all such anthologies have subsequently been based.

It was, in fact, only in the 1820s that the term 'nursery rhymes' came into use. Before that, these verses were simply known as 'songs' or 'ditties' and, in the 18th century, 'Tommy Thumb' songs or 'Mother Goose' melodies. It is by the latter title, obviously older than the British 'nursery rhymes', that any collection of these verses for children is still known in America. Who Mother Goose was, or why the rhymes were so called has never been satisfactorily explained, although 'Mother Goose' as teller of nursery tales was certainly familiar in France in the seventeenth century, and more so after the publication in 1798 of Charles Perrault's *Tales of My Mother Goose*, which contained the stories 'Little Red Riding Hood', 'Puss in Boots', 'Bluebeard', 'Sleeping Beauty', 'Cinderella', 'Little Tom Thumb' and a couple of others.

How old are some of these nursery rhymes? Halliwell clearly pointed out that no manuscript source is earlier than the reign of Henry VIII but, since so few of the rhymes were recorded before the 19th century, this is not particularly significant. Although they were passed on from generation to generation, the majority of these rhymes were not, in the first place, composed for children. Certainly, of those that date from before 1800, probably only counting-out rhymes, lullabies and those accompanying infant games were specifically for the nursery; the rest were adapted from old ballads or folksongs, street cries, proverbs, prayers or may possibly be remnants of ancient customs and rituals. As far as we can tell, it seems that at least a few of them would have been known in Shakespeare's day, perhaps about a quarter familiar in Charles I's reign and the others added thereafter.

As early as 1641 one writer complained that many of the rhymes repeated by children were unsavoury, and in another extraordinary example of misdirected labour, published in 1952, we are told of the incidence in nursery rhymes of (among other unpleasant happenings): death – by murder, decapitation, squeezing, shrivelling, starvation, hanging, drowning, etc; stealing and general dishonesty; maiming of human beings and animals; physical violence; lunacy; drunkenness; cursing and even racial discrimination. The author goes on to state that 'expressions of fear, weeping, moans of anguish, biting, pain and evidence of supreme selfishness may be found on almost every other page.' The possession in the nursery of many songs and rhymes quite unfit for childish ears is not as extraordinary as it may seem. From Elizabethan times to the early 19th century, children were rarely treated as anything other than miniature adults. Their dress and daily routine differed only slightly from that of their parents. Thus, the playing by moonlight we encounter in 'Boys and girls come out to play' simply indicates that, at that time, children kept the same late hours as adults. It is certain, too, that they were familiar not only with bawdy language but also with what we now call improper behaviour.

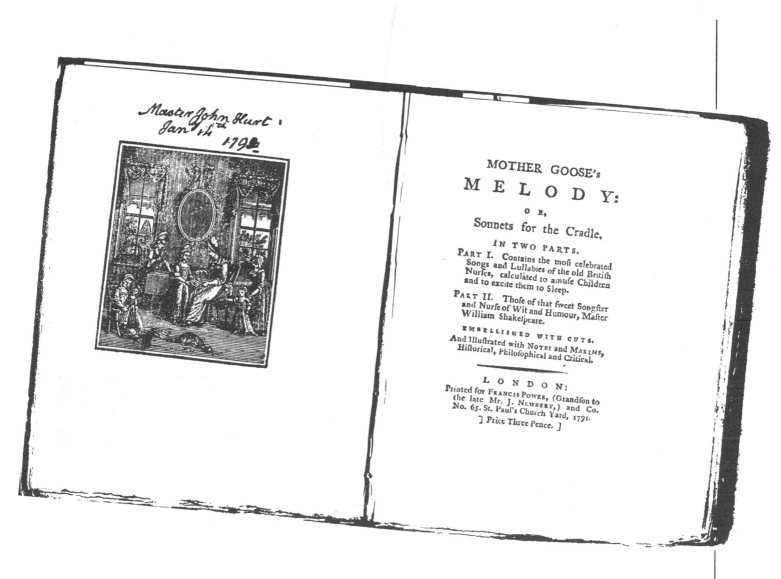

Sexual matters, drunkenness and other indelicacies would have left children unabashed, and in ages when infant mortality was high and man's life relatively short, death was no stranger; nor was violence or cruelty, since public beatings, the use of the stocks and other punishments could be witnessed all too frequently in the towns and countryside. That the children of past ages knew from an early age and at first hand about the harshness of life was, perhaps, no bad thing and that the rhymes that they repeated partly reflects this view is surely perfectly natural.

Yet wherever the English word is spoken these trivial verses have survived. Crooned by nursemaids and parents, their lilt and charm is often close to poetry. 'They have their own little beauty if looked at closely,' said Walter de la Mare. 'Many of them,' he went on, 'are tiny masterpieces of word craftsmanship . . . they are not only crammed with vivid little scenes and objects and living creatures, but, however fantastic and nonsensical they may be, they are a direct short cut into poetry itself.'

This frontispiece and title page is from the 1791 edition of Mother Goose's Melody, *the earliest known copy of this work which was first published in about 1765. There is some historical evidence to suggest that Oliver Goldsmith was the author of the preface and footnotes to these verses*

LITTLE BOY BLUE

It has been suggested that Little Boy Blue was intended to represent Thomas, Cardinal Wolsey, the son of an Ipswich butcher who became Henry VIII's Lord Chancellor, but fell from favour. As a child he probably did tend his father's sheep but there is no real reason for associating the rhyme with him and, as the editors of the *Oxford Dictionary of Nursery Rhymes* point out, it more closely resembles the lines from Act III, Scene VI of *King Lear*: 'Sleepest or wakest thou, jolly shepherd? / Thy sheep's in the corn; / And for one blast of thy minikin mouth / Thy sheep shall take no harm'.

Little Boy Blue, come blow your horn,
The cow's in the meadow, the sheep's in the corn;
Where is the boy who looks after the sheep?
He's under a haycock fast asleep.
Will you wake him? No, not I!
For if I do, he's sure to cry.

Thomas, Cardinal Wolsey (c1475-1530)

10

CURLY LOCKS, CURLY LOCKS

It has been suggested but not substantiated that 'Curly locks' is Charles II. One version of this was a popular courtship rhyme in Cumberland in the early 19th century.

Curly locks, Curly locks, wilt thou be mine?
Thou shalt not wash dishes, nor yet feed the swine;
But sit on a cushion and sew a fine seam,
And feed upon strawberries, sugar and cream.

THERE WAS A JOLLY MILLER ONCE

A mill has stood on the Dee at Chester since the 11th century and the legendary 'jolly miller' is said to have incurred the envy of Henry VIII because of his wealth and independence. The old mill on the Dee was burned down in 1895, a year after the death of the jolly miller's last descendant.

There was a jolly miller once,
Lived on the river Dee;
He worked and sang from morn till night,
No lark as blithe as he.
And this the burden of his song
Forever used to be,
I care for nobody, no! not I,
And nobody cares for me.

Bridge and mill on the river Dee, 1645

PETER, PETER, PUMPKIN EATER

The pumpkin is, curiously, a popular vegetable in children's literature, possibly because of its association with Halloween, when hollowed-out pumpkins are used to make the lanterns said to warn off evil spirits. It will be remembered, too, that Cinderella's coach was magically transformed from a pumpkin.

Peter, Peter, pumpkin eater,
Had a wife and couldn't keep her;
He put her in a pumpkin shell,
And there he kept her very well.

Peter, Peter, pumpkin eater,
Had another and didn't love her;
Peter learned to read and spell,
And then he loved her very well.

13

THREE BLIND MICE

A version of this very popular
round first appeared in 1609,
although it was not found in
children's literature before the
mid–19th century.

Three blind mice, see how they run!
They all ran after the farmer's wife,
Who cut off their tails with a carving knife,
Did you ever see such a thing in your life,
As three blind mice?

THREE BLIND MICE

BY A.M.SHAW

HICKORY, DICKORY, DOCK

This rhyme, like so many others, attempts to capture a sound – the ticking of a grandfather clock – in words. The rhyme was known from at least the middle of the 18th century and was a favourite of Sir Walter Scott's, who repeated it to one of his frequent visitors, the child (and diarist) Marjorie Fleming.

Hickory, dickory, dock,
The mouse ran up the clock.
The clock struck one,
The mouse ran down,
Hickory, dickory dock.

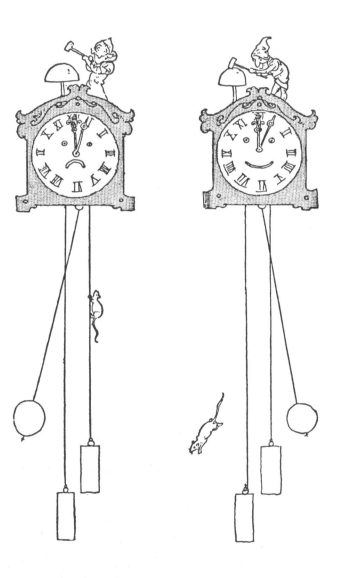

EENA, MEENA, MINA, MO

This counting-out rhyme, used to single out which, in a group of children, shall be 'it', is perhaps the most popular of such rhymes in the English-speaking world. There are similar versions of the first line in German and in Cornish dialect.

Eena, meena, mina, mo,
Catch a tiger by the toe;
If he squeals, let him go,
Eena, meena, mina, mo.

GEORGIE PORGIE

There are various historical contenders for this role. George I is one, George Villiers, Duke of Buckingham, another and popular tradition says Charles II. Although familiar since the late 19th century, this version of the rhyme does not seem to have been common in the nursery before about 1850.

Charles II (1630-85)

Georgie Porgie, pudding and pie,
Kissed the girls and made them cry;
When the boys came out to play,
Georgie Porgie ran away.

This is one of the most popular of all nursery rhymes and there was already speculation in Queen Anne's reign about the identity of this jolly monarch. According to the ancient chroniclers, a King Cole certainly ruled in Britain in the third century. He is said to have built Colchester and in the city a gravel pit of Roman origin is still known locally as 'King Cole's kitchen'. The 12th century chronicler, Geoffrey of Monmouth, states that Cole's daughter was skilled in music which could, perhaps, account for her father's appreciation of the art.

Old King Cole
Was a merry old soul,
And a merry old soul was he;
He called for his pipe,
And he called for his bowl,
And he called for his fiddlers three.

Every fiddler he had a fiddle,
And a very fine fiddle had he;
Oh, there's none so rare,
As can compare
With King Cole and his fiddlers three.

HARK, HARK, THE DOGS DO BARK

It is possible that this refers to the beggars of Tudor times when, out of a total population of under five million, 10,000 or more were out of work. The unfortunate vagabonds, mostly able-bodied men and women, roamed the countryside raiding lonely farms and cottages and openly begging for alms in the towns. The 'velvet gown' here would clearly have been stolen property. Another suggestion is that the beggars were the Dutchmen who came to England with William III in 1688, the 'one in a velvet gown' (as this line appears in some versions) being William III himself.

Hark, hark, the dogs do bark,
The beggars are coming to town;
Some in rags, and some in jags,
And some in velvet gowns.

22

OH, THE GRAND OLD DUKE OF YORK

The duke was Frederick Augustus, Duke of York and second son of George III. According to his biographer, Colonel Burne, there is no event in the Duke's military career 'which remotely resembles the operation described in the jingle', and it is probable that these lines were adapted by one of his detractors from the old rhyme: 'The king of France went up the hill with forty thousand men, / The king of France came down the hill and ne'er went up again'.

Oh, the grand old Duke of York,
He had ten thousand men:
He marched them up to the top of a hill,
And he marched them down again.
And when they were up, they were up,
And when they were down, they were down,
And when they were only half way up,
They were neither up nor down.

Frederick Augustus, Duke of York (1763-1827)

A WAS AN APPLE PIE

This popular rhyme for teaching the alphabet was well-known in the reign of Charles II, but was a particularly favourite method of instruction in the 19th century when it appeared in a large number of nursery rhyme books.

A was an apple pie,
B bit it,
C cut it,
D dealt it,
E eat it,
F fought for it,
G got it,
H had it,
I inspected it,
J jumped for it,
K kept it,
L longed for it,
M mourned for it,
N nodded at it,
O opened it,
P peeped in it,
Q quartered it,
R ran for it,
S stole it,
T took it,
U upset it,
V viewed it,
W wanted it,
X, Y, Z and ampersand
All wished for a piece in hand.

A was an
Apple pie

B
Bit it

C
Cut it

D
Dealt it

E
Eat it

F
Fought for it

G
Got it

H
Had it

I
Inspected it

J
Joined for it

K
Kept it

L
Longed for it

M
Mourned for it

N
Nodded at it

O
Opened it

P
Peeped in it

Q
Quartered it

R
Ran for it

S
Stole it

T
Took it

U
Upset it

V
Viewed it

W
Wanted it

XYZ and &
All wished for
a piece in hand

DING, DONG, BELL

Versions of this, one of the oldest of nursery rhymes, have existed since at least the late 16th century. Shakespeare uses 'Ding dong bell' as the burden of songs in *The Merchant of Venice*, Act III, Scene II: 'Let us all ring fancy's knell; / I'll begin it – Ding, dong, bell'. And in *The Tempest*, Act I, Scene II: 'Sea-nymphs hourly ring his knell: / Hark! now I hear them – Ding, dong, bell'.

Ding, dong, bell,
Pussy's in the well.
Who put her in?
Little Johnny Green.
Who pulled her out?
Little Tommy Stout.
What a naughty boy was that
To try to drown poor pussy cat,
Who never did him any harm
And killed the mice in his father's barn.

Ding, dong, bell,
Pussy's in the well!
Who put her in?
Little Tommy Green,
Who pulled her out?
Little Johnny Stout,
What a naughty boy was that,
To try and drown poor Pussy-cat!

RIDE A COCK-HORSE TO BANBURY CROSS

The lady here has been variously identified as Elizabeth I, Lady Godiva and a 17th century noblewoman called Celia Fiennes, whose family lived at Broughton Castle near Banbury, and who made many rides on horseback through England after 1697. The big cross at Banbury was destroyed in 1601 in a fit of Puritan zeal and the 'bells on her toes' refers to the 15th century custom of attaching bells to the tapering toes of each shoe.

Ride a cock–horse to Banbury Cross,
To see a fine lady upon a white horse;
With rings on her fingers and bells on her toes,
She shall have music wherever she goes.

Mother GOOSE's Melody. 33

RIDE a cock horse
To *Banbury* crofs,
To fee what *Tommy* can buy;
A penny white loaf,
A penny white cake,
And a two-penny apple-pye.

There's a good boy, eat up your pye and hold your tongue; for filence is the fign of wifdom.

COCK

DOCTOR FOSTER WENT TO GLOUCESTER

A popular tradition in the West Country suggests that Doctor Foster was Edward I whose horse, on one of his visits to the city, floundered in the mud of a Gloucester street. So deep was the mud that planks had to be laid down before the horse could regain its footing and Edward, distressed and angered by the incident, vowed he would never visit Gloucester again.

Doctor Foster went to Gloucester
In a shower of rain;
He stepped in a puddle, right up to his middle,
And never went there again.

Gloucester. From a 17th century print

29

BOYS AND GIRLS, COME OUT TO PLAY

This popular song was known in adult literature in the early 18th century and probably dates from the middle of the 17th century. It is only in relatively modern times (and largely in Anglo-Saxon countries) that children have been sent to bed soon after dark. In the 17th century it would not have been unnatural for children, who were dressed and treated as miniature adults, to be playing by moonlight.

Boys and girls, come out to play,
The moon doth shine as bright as day,
Leave your supper, and leave your sleep,
And come with your playfellows into the street.
Come with a whoop, come with a call,
Come with a good will, or come not at all.
Up the ladder and down the wall,
A halfpenny loaf will serve us all.
You find milk, and I'll find flour,
And we'll have pudding in half an hour.

Girls and boys come out to play,
The moon doth shine as bright as day;
Come with a whoop, and come with a call,
Come with a good will or not at all.

1. Girls and boys come out to play, The moon doth shine as bright as day; Come with a whoop, and come with a call, Come with a good will or not at all.
2. Leave your sup-per, and leave your sleep; Come to your playfellows in the street; Up the lad-der and down the wall, A pen-ny loaf will serve you all.

HEY DIDDLE, DIDDLE

This charming and immensely popular nonsense rhyme is very ancient. According to a play written by Thomas Preston in 1569 'hey diddle diddle' was a new dance accompanied by a tune on the fiddle. Some commentators have suggested that Elizabeth I is the Cat and Robert Dudley, Earl of Leicester, the Dog ('he is like my little lap-dog . . .' she once said of him). Others claim that it refers, respectively, to Catherine of Aragon, Catherine the Great, Caton, a supposed governor of Calais called Caton le fidèle, and the game of cat or trap ball, a popular tavern game. The editors of the *Oxford Dictionary of Nursery Rhymes* suggest that most of this is nonsense and add 'the sanest observation on this rhyme seems to have been made by Sir Henry Reid, "I prefer to think", he says, "that it commemorates the athletic lunacy to which the strange conspiracy of the cat and the fiddle incited the cow"'.

Hey diddle, diddle,
The cat and the fiddle,
The cow jumped over the moon;
The little dog laughed
To see such fun,
And the dish ran away with the spoon.

WHO KILLED COCK ROBIN?

Many believe that this tale dates at least from the 14th century, indicated by the rhyming of 'shovel' with 'Owl' when the pronunciation of the former was 'shouell'. It has also been suggested that it is a rendering in rhyme of some early myth, possibly that of the death of Balder, the Norse god of summer sunlight, slain by Hoder at the instigation of Loki. Others see a parallel with the intrigues which brought the downfall of Robert Walpole's ministry (popularly known as the Robinocracy) in 1742. Certainly, the earliest known recording of the rhyme (c.1774) coincides with Walpole's downfall and it is possible that the old rhyme was resurrected or rewritten at this time. The 'link' here means a torch, and the 'bull', a bullfinch.

Sir Robert Walpole, 1st Earl of Orford (1676-1745)

Who killed Cock Robin?
I, said the Sparrow,
With my bow and arrow,
I killed Cock Robin.

Who saw him die?
I, said the Fly,
With my little eye,
I saw him die.

Who caught his blood?
I, said the Fish,
With my little dish,
I caught his blood.

Who'll make his shroud?
I, said the Beetle,
With my thread and needle,
I'll make his shroud.

Who'll dig his grave?
I, said the Owl,
With my spade and shovel,
I'll dig his grave.

Who'll be the parson?
I, said the Rook,
With my little book,
I'll be the parson.

33

Who'll be the clerk?
I, said the Lark,
If it's not in the dark,
I'll be the clerk.

Who'll carry him to the grave?
I, said the Kite,
If it's not in the night,
I'll carry him to the grave.

Who'll carry the link?
I, said the Linnet,
I'll fetch it in a minute,
I'll carry the link.

Who'll be the chief mourner?
I, said the Dove,
For I mourn for my love,
I'll be the chief mourner.

Who'll bear the pall?
We, says the Wren,
Both the cock and the hen,
We'll bear the pall.

Who'll sing a psalm?
I, said the Thrush,
As she sat in a bush,
I'll sing a psalm.

Who'll toll the bell?
I, said the Bull,
Because I can pull,
So, Cock Robin, farewell.

All the birds of the air,
Fell a-sighing and a-sobbing,
When they heard the bell tolling
For poor Cock Robin.

POOR COCK ROBIN.

HIS DEATH AND BURIAL.

Who kill'd Cock Robin?

Who saw him die?

BAA, BAA, BLACK SHEEP

This rhyme has been known for some 200 years and was used by Kipling in 1888 for his story of the same title.

Baa, baa, black sheep,
Have you any wool?
Yes, sir, yes, sir,
Three bags full;
One for the master,
And one for the dame,
And one for the little boy
Who lives down the lane.

Mother **GOOSE's** Melody, 59

BAH, bah, black fheep,
Have you any wool?
Yes, marry have I,
Three bags full;
One for my mafter,
One for my dame,
But none for the little boy
Who cries in the lane.

Maxim.

Bad habits are eafier conquered to day than to-morrow.
ROBIN

THERE WAS A LITTLE GIRL

A great deal has been written, particularly in the U.S., about the origins of this rhyme. It is popularly supposed, and indeed probable, that Henry Wadsworth Longfellow wrote it for his daughter, Edith, on a day when she refused to have her hair curled.

There was a little girl, and she had a little curl
Right in the middle of her forehead;
When she was good she was very, very good,
But when she was bad she was horrid.

HOT CROSS BUNS!

This street cry, which has been sung for several centuries, was chanted on Good Friday morning when hot cross buns were, and still are, eaten. Sacred, spiced cakes, cooked on special festive days, were probably introduced to Britain by the Romans.

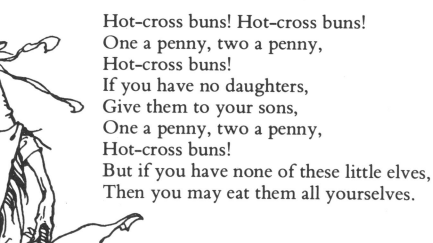

Hot-cross buns! Hot-cross buns!
One a penny, two a penny,
Hot-cross buns!
If you have no daughters,
Give them to your sons,
One a penny, two a penny,
Hot-cross buns!
But if you have none of these little elves,
Then you may eat them all yourselves.

A FROG HE WOULD A-WOOING GO

This ballad can be traced back to
the mid-16th century, and in one
or other of its versions has been
consistently popular. This, the
most recent and best-known,
dates from the early 19th
century. It has been suggested
that the 'rowley powley' of the
refrain refers to a plump chicken.

A frog he would a-wooing go,
Heigh ho! says Rowley,
Whether his mother would let him or no.
With a rowley, powley, gammon and spinach,
Heigh ho! Says Anthony Rowley.

So off he sets with his opera hat,
Heigh ho! says Rowley,
And on the road he met a rat.
With a rowley, powley, gammon and spinach,
Heigh ho! says Anthony Rowley.

Pray, Mister Rat, will you go with me?
Heigh ho! says Rowley,
Kind Mistress Mousey for to see?
With a rowley, powley, gammon and spinach,
Heigh ho! says Anthony Rowley.

They came to the door of Mousey's hall,
Heigh ho! says Rowley,
They gave a loud knock and they gave a loud call.
With a rowley, powley, gammon and spinach,
Heigh ho! says Anthony Rowley.

Pray, Mistress Mouse, are you within?
Heigh ho! says Rowley,
Oh yes, kind sirs, I'm sitting to spin.
With a rowley, powley, gammon and spinach,
Heigh ho! says Anthony Rowley.

Pray, Mistress Mouse, will you give us some beer?
Heigh ho! says Rowley,
For Froggy and I are fond of good cheer.
With a rowley, powley, gammon and spinach,
Heigh ho! says Anthony Rowley.

Pray, Mister Frog, will you give us a song?
Heigh ho! says Rowley,
Let it be something that's not very long.
With a rowley, powley, gammon and spinach,
Heigh ho! says Anthony Rowley.

Indeed, Mistress Mouse, replied Mister Frog,
Heigh ho! says Rowley,
A cold has made me as hoarse as a dog.
With a rowley, powley, gammon and spinach,
Heigh ho! says Anthony Rowley.

Since you have a cold, Mister Frog, Mousey said,
Heigh ho! says Rowley,
I'll sing you a song that I have just made.
With a rowley, powley, gammon and spinach,
Heigh ho! says Anthony Rowley.

But while they were all a–merry–making,
Heigh ho! says Rowley,
A cat and her kittens came tumbling in.
With a rowley, powley, gammon and spinach,
Heigh ho! says Anthony Rowley.

The cat she seized the rat by the crown,
Heigh ho! says Rowley,
The kittens they pulled the little mouse down.
With a rowley, powley, gammon and spinach,
Heigh ho! says Anthony Rowley.

This put Mister Frog in a terrible fright,
Heigh ho! says Rowley,
He took up his hat and he wished them good-night.
With a rowley, powley, gammon and spinach,
Heigh ho! says Anthony Rowley.

But as Froggy was crossing over a brook,
Heigh ho! says Rowley,
A lily-white duck came and gobbled him up.
With a rowley, powley, gammon and spinach,
Heigh ho! says Anthony Rowley.

So there was an end of one, two, three,
Heigh ho! says Rowley,
The rat, the mouse and the little frog-ee.
With a rowley, powley, gammon and spinach,
Heigh ho! says Anthony Rowley.

OH DEAR, WHAT CAN THE MATTER BE?

This charming song, first printed at the end of the 18th century, has remained popular ever since. It was probably first introduced to the nursery by nursemaids who plaintively sang it to their young charges.

Oh dear, what can the matter be?
Dear, dear, what can the matter be?
Oh dear, what can the matter be?
Johnny's so long at the fair.

He promised he'd buy me a fairing should please me,
And then for a kiss, oh! he vowed he would tease
    me,
He promised he'd bring me a bunch of blue ribbons
To tie up my bonny brown hair.

Oh dear, what can the matter be?
Dear, dear what can the matter be?
Oh dear, what can the matter be?
Johnny's so long at the fair.

He promised to buy me a pair of sleeve buttons,
A pair of new garters that cost him but two pence,
He promised he'd bring me a bunch of blue ribbons
To tie up my bonny brown hair.

Oh dear, what can the matter be?
Dear, dear, what can the matter be?
Oh dear, what can the matter be?
Johnny's so long at the fair.

He promised he'd bring me a basket of posies,
A garland of lilies, a garland of roses,
A little straw hat, to set off the blue ribbons
That tie up my bonny brown hair.

GOOSEY, GOOSEY GANDER

This rhyme, in its present form, is amalgamated with 'Old Daddy Long-Legs', only the first four lines occurring in the original version known in the 18th century. The two were combined sometime at the beginning of the 19th century.

Goosey, goosey gander,
Whither shall I wander?
Upstairs and downstairs
And in my lady's chamber.
There I met an old man
Who would not say his prayers.
I took him by the left leg
And threw him down the stairs.

GOOSEY GOOSEY GANDER

BYAM·SHAW

STAIRS·&·DOWNSTAIRS·&·IN·MY·LADY'S·CHAMBER

LITTLE BO-PEEP

One of the most familiar of all nursery rhymes, this is first recorded in the early 19th century, although the game of 'bo-peep', a form of hide and seek or even a simple infant amusement of concealing a baby's head for an instant and then revealing it, is referred to in Elizabethan literature.

Little Bo-peep has lost her sheep,
And doesn't know where to find them;
Leave them alone, and they'll come home,
Bringing their tails behind them.

Little Bo-peep fell fast asleep,
And dreamt she heard them bleating;
But when she awoke, she found it a joke,
For they were still a-fleeting.

Then up she took her little crook,
Determined her to find them;
She found them indeed, but it made her heart bleed,
For they'd left their tails behind them.

It happened one day, as Bo-peep did stray
Into a meadow hard by,
There she espied their tails side by side,
All hung on a tree to dry.

She heaved a sigh, and wiped her eye,
And over the hillocks went rambling,
And tried what she could, as a shepherdess should,
To tack again each to its lambkin.

HUMPTY DUMPTY

This extremely popular rhyme is, of course, a riddle. Humpty Dumpty was an egg and having fallen and broken could not be put together again. It is thought that the rhyme is very ancient indeed and it is known elsewhere in Europe in substantially the same form. The character of Humpty Dumpty has been immortalized by Lewis Carroll in *Through the Looking Glass*, where the last line is given as 'Couldn't put Humpty Dumpty in his place again' – which, observed Alice, 'is much too long for poetry'.

Humpty Dumpty sat on a wall,
Humpty Dumpty had a great fall;
All the King's horses and all the King's men
Couldn't put Humpty together again.

NOW I LAY ME DOWN TO SLEEP

This famous children's prayer was widely disseminated in the 18th century on both sides of the Atlantic. An amusing parody of it also exists: 'Now I lay me down to sleep, A bag of peanuts at my feet / If I should die before I wake, Give them to my sister Kate.'

Now I lay me down to sleep,
I pray the Lord my soul to keep;
And if I die before I wake,
I pray the Lord my soul to take.

SEE-SAW, MARGERY DAW

Margery, a name used by poor country folk in the 18th and 19th centuries, and Daw, meaning an untidy person, a sluggard or slut, suggest that this creature, whoever she may have been, was hardly a respectable female. The rhyme is traditionally repeated by children playing on a see-saw and may possibly have originally been sung by sawyers to keep the rhythm of a two-handled saw.

See-saw, Margery Daw,
Jacky shall have a new master;
Jacky shall have but a penny a day,
Because he can't work any faster.

Although Mother Hubbard was a stock nursery rhyme character and known since the 16th century at least, this version of the rhyme was written in 1804 by Sarah Catherine Martin, daughter of Sir Henry Martin and an early love of Prince William Henry (later William IV). *The Comic Adventures of Mother Hubbard and her Dog*, published the following year, was an immediate success with upwards of 10,000 copies sold in a few months, followed by numerous reprints. Miss Martin, it seems, wrote the rhyme after her future brother-in-law, John Pollexfen Bastard, MP for Kitley, Devon, had chided her for chattering while he was writing a letter and urged her to run away and write 'one of your stupid little rhymes'. The archaic rhyming of 'laughing' with 'coffin' suggests that Miss Martin may have used an early version of the rhyme as the basis for her verses.

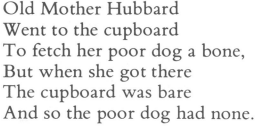

Old Mother Hubbard
Went to the cupboard
To fetch her poor dog a bone,
But when she got there
The cupboard was bare
And so the poor dog had none.

She went to the baker's
To buy him some bread,
But when she came back
The poor dog was dead.

She went to the joiner's
To buy him a coffin,
But when she came back
The poor dog was laughing.

She took a clean dish
To get him some tripe,
But when she came back
He was smoking a pipe.

She went to the fishmonger's
To buy him some fish,
But when she came back
He was licking the dish.

She went to the ale-house
To get him some beer,
But when she came back
The dog sat in a chair.

She went to the tavern
For white wine and red,
But when she came back
The dog stood on his head.

She went to the hatter's
To buy him a hat,
But when she came back
He was feeding the cat.

She went to the barber's
To buy him a wig,
But when she came back
He was dancing a jig.

She went to the fruiterer's
To buy him some fruit,
But when she came back
He was playing the flute.

She went to the tailor's
To buy him a coat,
But when she came back
He was riding a goat.

She went to the cobbler's
To buy him some shoes,
But when she came back
He was reading the news.

She went to the sempstress
To buy him some linen,
But when she came back
The dog was a-spinning.

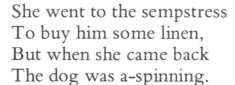

She went to the hosier's
To buy him some hose,
But when she came back
He was dressed in his clothes.

The dame made a curtsey,
The dog made a bow;
The dame said, Your servant
The dog said, Bow-wow.

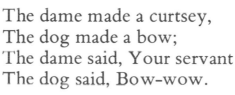

I HAD A LITTLE NUT TREE

It is thought that this contains a direct reference to the visit of Juana of Castile, daughter of Ferdinand and Isabella of Spain, to Henry VII's court in 1506. Both Henry and Juana had recently been widowed and, in pursuit of an alliance with Spain, it was thought that a match between the couple might be arranged. However, 'Mad' Juana was clearly not in her right mind and the plan was abandoned.

Detail from a painting of Juana of Castile over the bier of her dead husband, Philip the Handsome

I had a little nut tree, nothing would it bear
But a silver nutmeg and a golden pear;
The King of Spain's daughter came to visit me,
And all was because of my little nut tree.
I skipped over water, I danced over sea,
And all the birds in the air couldn't catch me.

ORANGES AND LEMONS

The church referred to here is either St Clement's in Eastcheap, near the wharves where citrus fruit was unloaded, or St Clement Danes, a Wren church erected in 1680 (much has been written in favour of both). St Martin's is probably St Martin's Lane in the City, where the moneylenders used to live. The Old Bailey, built on the site of the old Newgate Prison, does not possess a bell but the bell of St Sepulchre's opposite was traditionally rung when prisoners were about to be executed. Shoreditch, where a church once stood, is just outside the City walls. The bells of Stepney, also outside the City walls, were probably those of St Dunstan's. The famous Bow bells are those of St Mary le Bow in Cheapside, the ones that told Dick Wittington to 'turn again' and within whose sound a true Londoner, a Cockney, is born. The game played to this song ends in a tug-o-war between the 'oranges' and 'lemons', these having been determined by two players who form an arch and successively 'chop' each member of the group who then decides which side he will be on.

ST CLEMENT DANES, STRAND

Oranges and lemons,
Say the bells of St Clement's.

You owe me five farthings,
Say the bells of St Martin's.

When will you pay me?
Say the bells at Old Bailey.

When I grow rich,
Say the bells at Shoreditch.

Pray, when will that be?
Say the bells at Stepney.

I'm sure I don't know,
Says the great bell at Bow.

Here comes a candle to light you to bed,
And here comes a chopper to chop off your head.

THREE WISE MEN OF GOTHAM

For some 500 years the village of Gotham near Nottingham has been considered a town of fools – the 'foles of gotyam' are mentioned in a manuscript as early as 1450. Legend has it that the reputation originated in King John's reign. The king expressed his intention to pass through Gotham fields on his way to Nottingham, but in those days any thoroughfare through which the king passed thereafter became a public road. The Gothamites, determined to avert this, engaged in a number of idiotic pursuits. Some tried to drown an eel in a pond, others tried to trap a cuckoo and so have perpetual summer by building a hedge around it. The king's outriders, observing such lunatic behaviour, were convinced that the village was peopled by madmen. The king, so warned, took another route – the 'wise' men of Gotham thus achieving their aims.

Three wise men of Gotham
Went to sea in a bowl;
If the bowl had been stronger,
My story would have been longer.

Mother GOOSE's Melody. 21

THREE wife men of *Gotham,*
They went to fea in a bowl,
And if the bowl had been ftronger,
My fong had been longer.

It is long enough. Never lament
the lofs of what is not worth having.
Boyle.

B 3   THERE

POLLY PUT THE KETTLE ON

This rhyme has been known
since the late 18th century. Polly
was a pet name for Mary, and
Sukey for Susan. Dickens has
Grip, the raven, quote it in
Barnaby Rudge.

Polly put the kettle on,
Polly put the kettle on,
Polly put the kettle on,
We'll all have tea.

Sukey take it off again,
Sukey take it off again,
Sukey take it off again,
They've all gone away.

HUSH-A-BYE, BABY

No one is certain of the age of this immensely familiar lullaby although it has been suggested by one authority that it refers to the ancient Egyptian god of the sky, Horus, as a child. More likely, it tells of the age-old custom of hanging a baby's cradle on the bough of a tree to let the wind do the rocking, a practice common in hop gardens when the women helped with the picking. Another legend suggests that a Pilgrim youth who went to America in the *Mayflower* composed this after seeing the American Indians rock their children in birchbark cradles.

Hush-a-bye, baby, on the tree top,
When the wind blows, the cradle will rock;
When the bough breaks, the cradle will fall,
Down will come baby, cradle and all.

BOBBY SHAFTO

Sir Walter Scott described this as 'an old Northumbrian ditty'. The original Bobby Shafto is said to have lived at Hollybrook, County Wicklow and died in 1737. The last verse, however, refers to Robert Shafto of Whitworth Hall, near Durham, a Parliamentary candidate in the 1761 elections and said to be uncommonly handsome.

Robert Shafto of Whitworth

Bobby Shafto's gone to sea,
Silver buckles at his knee;
He'll come back and marry me,
Bonny Bobby Shafto!

Bobby Shafto's fat and fair,
Combing down his yellow hair;
He's my love for evermore,
Bonny Bobby Shafto!

Bobby Shafto's looking out,
All his ribbons flew about;
All the ladies gave a shout,
Hey for Bobby Shafto!

JACK BE NIMBLE

Candle-leaping has long been practised in England both as a sport and as a way of telling fortunes. It was believed that the person who could jump over a lighted candle, placed in the centre of a room, without extinguishing the flame was assured of good luck for the following year. It was a popular custom particularly among the lacemakers of Wendover in Buckinghamshire on the feast day of their patron saint, St Catherine, on November 25th.

Jack be nimble,
Jack be quick,
Jack jump over
The candlestick.

DANCE TO YOUR DADDY

This dandling song is particularly popular in Scotland and the North Country, often with an additional verse: 'Baby shall have an apple, / Baby shall have a plum, / Baby shall have a rattle when Daddy comes home'.

Dance to your daddy,
My little babby,
Dance to your daddy,
My little lamb.
You shall have a fishy
In a little dishy,
You shall have a fishy
When the boat comes in.

LADYBIRD, LADYBIRD, FLY AWAY HOME

This is recited when a ladybird lights on one's hand or arm, since to kill these pretty creatures is considered bad luck. The ladybird (Our Lady's bird) seems to have had some religious significance since ancient times and similar incantations appear in other European languages.

Ladybird, ladybird, fly away home,
Your house is on fire, your children are gone;
All but one and her name is Ann,
And she crept under the pudding-pan.

HOW MANY MILES TO BABYLON?

This rhyme dates from Elizabethan times at least and may possibly be older. 'Can I get there by candlelight?' was a common saying in the 16th and 17th centuries. 'Babylon' may be a corruption of Babyland but its hint of the exotic comes from the association with the magnificent city of the ancient East, whose luxurious gardens were one of the seven wonders of the ancient world. The mysterious and magical quality of this rhyme is still as powerful today as it was to Stevenson, Kipling and Lewis Carroll, who all referred to it.

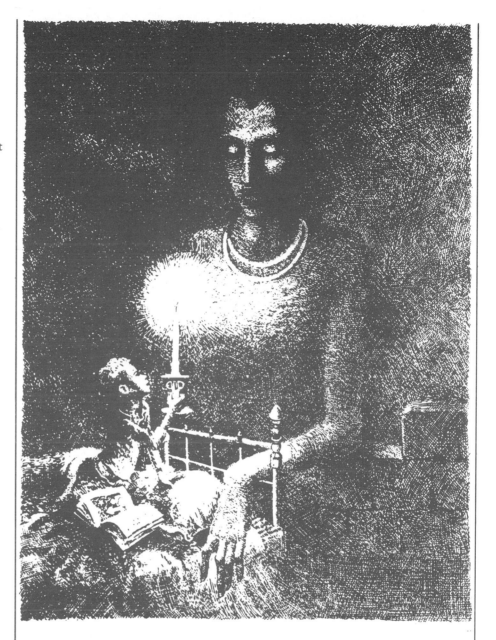

How many miles to Babylon?
Three score and ten.
Can I get there by candle-light?
Yes, and back again.
If your heels are nimble and light,
You may get there by candle-light.

JACK SPRAT

In the 16th and 17th centuries Jack Sprat or Prat was the common name for a dwarf and indeed the rhyme, in various versions, is first recorded in the 17th century. One refers to an Archdeacon Pratt, presumably a contemporary clergyman of dwarf-like proportions, and his wife, Joan.

Jack Sprat could eat no fat,
His wife could eat no lean,
And so, between them both, you see,
They licked the platter clean.

Jack Sprat could eat no fat,
His wife could eat no lean,
And so betwixt them both
They lick'd the platter clean.

THIRTY DAYS HATH SEPTEMBER

This rhymed memory-aid, one of the best-known in the language, goes back at least to the early 17th century. It is also found in both Latin and French.

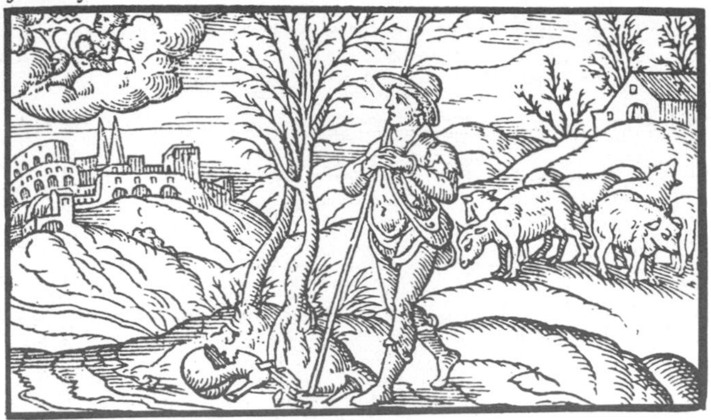

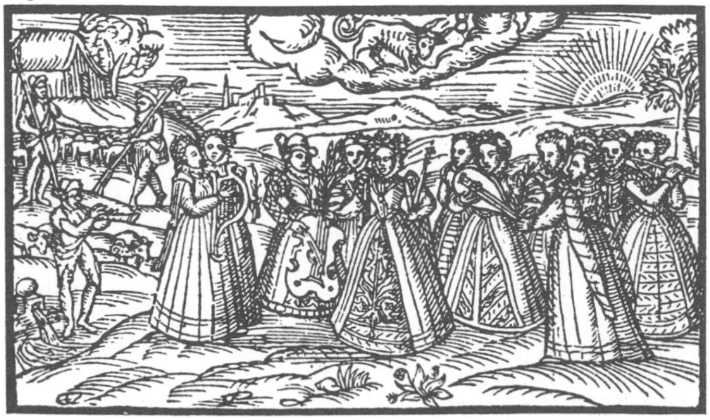

January

February

March

April

Thirty days hath September,
April, June and November;
All the rest have thirty-one,
Excepting February alone,
And that has twenty-eight days clear
And twenty-nine in each leap year.

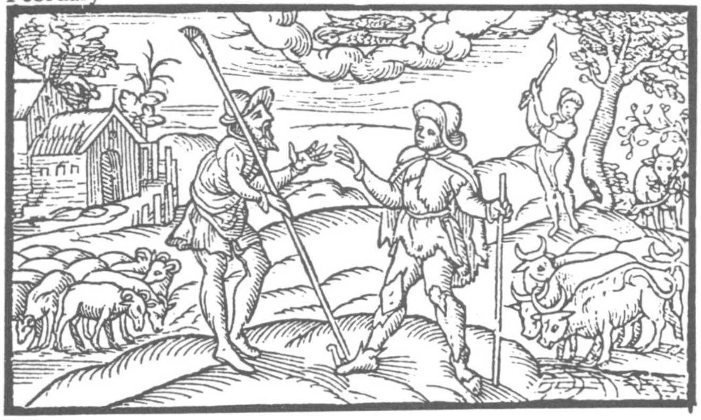

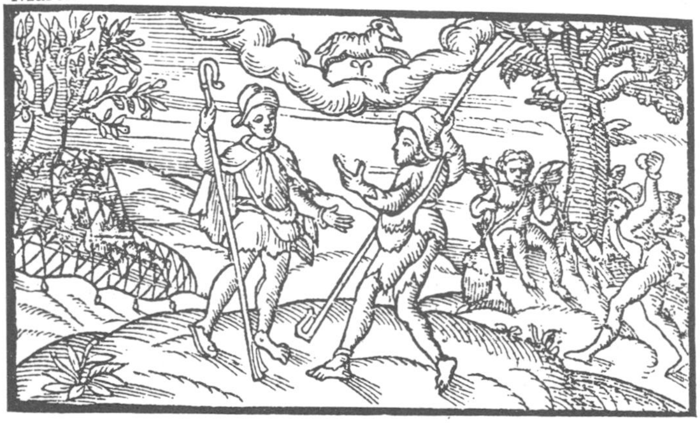

Illustrations to Spenser's Shepherd's Calendar, *1579*

May

September

June

October

July

November

August

December

ONE, TWO, BUCKLE MY SHOE

This counting rhyme may have originally gone up to 30. It was said to have been used as early as 1780 in Wrentham, Mass., and forms of it are common in Germany, France, Holland and Turkey.

One, two,
Buckle my shoe;
Three, four,
Shut the door;
Five, six,
Pick up sticks;
Seven, eight,
Lay them straight;
Nine, ten,
A big fat hen;

Eleven, twelve,
Dig and delve;
Thirteen, fourteen,
Maids a-courting;
Fifteen, sixteen,
Maids in the kitchen;
Seventeen, eighteen,
Maids in waiting;
Nineteen, twenty,
My plate's empty.

19, 20.

Nineteen, Twenty.
My plate is empty.

TWINKLE, TWINKLE, LITTLE STAR

This familiar rhyme was written by Jane Taylor (1783-1824) and published in 1806. With her sister, Ann, she was a popular authoress of nursery poems. Lewis Carroll's Mad Hatter parodied the rhyme in *Alice in Wonderland* with: 'Twinkle, twinkle, little bat! / How I wonder what you're at! / Up above the world you fly, / Like a tea-tray in the sky'.

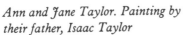
Ann and Jane Taylor. Painting by their father, Isaac Taylor

Twinkle, twinkle, little star,
How I wonder what you are!
Up above the moon so high,
Like a diamond in the sky.

WEE WILLIE WINKIE

In Jacobite songs Wee Willie Winkie was a nickname for William III. This rhyme, however, first published in 1841, was written by William Miller (1810–72) 'the laureate of the nursery' and it is unlikely that he intended it to have any political significance.

William III (1650-1702)

Wee Willie Winkie runs through the town,
Upstairs and downstairs in his nightgown,
Rapping at the window, crying through the lock,
Are the children all in bed, for now it's eight o'clock?

MARY HAD A LITTLE LAMB

The first of these verses is probably the best-known four-line verse in the language. The rhyme was written by Mrs Sarah Joseph Hale of Boston in 1830, apparently about an incident which was 'partly true'.

Mary had a little lamb,
Its fleece was white as snow;
And everywhere that Mary went
The lamb was sure to go.

It followed her to school one day,
That was against the rule;
It made the children laugh and play
To see a lamb at school.

And so the teacher turned it out,
But still it lingered near;
And waited patiently about
Till Mary did appear.

Why does the lamb love Mary so?
The eager children cry;
Why, Mary loves the lamb, you know,
The teacher did reply.

THIS LITTLE PIG WENT TO MARKET

This is surely the most common of toe games, and has been for well over a century.

This little pig went to market,
This little pig stayed at home,
This little pig had roast beef,
This little pig had none,
And this little pig cried, Wee, wee, wee,
All the way home.

TAFFY WAS A WELSHMAN

This is one of several versions of this rhyme. Taffy, the Welsh pronunciation of Davy, has long been the nickname given by Englishmen to the Welshman. Moreover, baiting the Welsh on St David's Day (March 1st) is an age-old custom, notably recorded by Shakespeare in *Henry V* (Act V, Scene I), when the Welsh captain Fluellen is forced by Pistol to eat a leek on March 1st.

Taffy was a Welshman, Taffy was a thief;
Taffy came to my house and stole a piece of beef.
I went to Taffy's house, Taffy wasn't home;
Taffy came to my house and stole a marrow-bone.
I went to Taffy's house, Taffy wasn't in;
Taffy came to my house and stole a silver pin.
I went to Taffy's house, Taffy was in bed;
I took up the marrow-bone and flung it at his head.

TINKER, TAILOR, SOLDIER, SAILOR

This formula, used by children with counters of some sort – cherry stones, daisy petals or waistcoat buttons – determines what the child shall be 'when he grows up'.

Tinker, tailor, soldier, sailor,
Rich man, poor man, beggar man, thief.

THERE WAS A CROOKED MAN

It has been suggested by one scholar that the crooked man may have been General Sir Alexander Leslie of Scotland, one of those who signed the Covenant during Charles I's reign, securing the religious and political freedom of Scotland. The 'crooked sixpence' would thus be Charles I, and the 'crooked stile' the English/ Scottish border. That the English and Scots reached agreement, after Leslie had crossed the border and seized Newcastle in 1640, is implicit in 'they all lived together in a little crooked house'.

There was a crooked man, and he walked a crooked
    mile,
He found a crooked sixpence against a crooked stile;
He bought a crooked cat, which caught a crooked
    mouse,
And they all lived together in a little crooked house.

BYE, BABY BUNTING

Bunting is an early form of endearment, known in the 17th century.

Bye, baby bunting,
Daddy's gone a-hunting,
To get a little skin
To wrap the baby bunting in.

FOR WANT OF A NAIL

This proverb has been known since the 17th century when a French military proverb 'the loss of a nail, the loss of an army' was also familiar.

For want of a nail, the shoe was lost,
For want of a shoe, the horse was lost,
For want of a horse, the rider was lost,
For want of a rider, the battle was lost,
For want of a battle, the kingdom was lost,
And all for the want of a horseshoe nail.

MATTHEW, MARK, LUKE, AND JOHN

This prayer is very old and may have its origins in half–Celtic magic and half–Christian ritual. Originally known as the 'White Paternoster' it was, over a century ago, more familiar in many English country districts than the Lord's Prayer.

Matthew, Mark, Luke, and John,
Bless the bed that I lie on.
Four corners to my bed,
Four angels round my head;
One to watch, one to pray,
And two to bear my soul away.

LONDON BRIDGE HAS FALLEN DOWN

The game played to this song could date back to 14th century Florence and certainly versions of it have been widespread throughout Europe for many centuries. It has been suggested that this rhyme refers to the actual destruction of London Bridge by King Olaf and his Norsemen in the 11th century. Since early times various superstitions have been associated with both the erection and collapse of bridges, the most notable being that water spirits object to bridges as an invasion of their privacy. Consequently, human sacrifices, especially children, have been buried in a bridge's foundations, supposedly to serve as guardian spirits. A bridge demolished in Bremen in the last century revealed the skeleton of one such child.

London Bridge about 1616

London Bridge has fallen down,
Fallen down, fallen down,
London Bridge has fallen down,
My fair Lady.

Build it up with wood and clay,
Wood and clay, wood and clay,
Build it up with wood and clay,
My fair Lady.

Wood and clay will wash away,
Wash away, wash away,
Wood and clay will wash away,
My fair Lady.

Build it up with bricks and mortar,
Bricks and mortar, bricks and mortar,
Build it up with bricks and mortar,
My fair Lady.

Bricks and mortar will not stay,
Will not stay, will not stay,
Bricks and mortar will not stay,
My fair Lady.

Build it up with iron and steel,
Iron and steel, iron and steel,
Build it up with iron and steel,
My fair Lady.

Iron and steel will bend and bow,
Bend and bow, bend and bow,
Iron and steel will bend and bow,
My fair Lady.

Build it up with silver and gold,
Silver and gold, silver and gold,
Build it up with silver and gold,
My fair Lady.

Silver and gold will be stolen away,
Stolen away, stolen away,
Silver and gold will be stolen away,
My fair Lady.

Set a man to watch all night,
Watch all night, watch all night,
Set a man to watch all night,
My fair Lady.

Suppose the man should fall asleep,
Fall asleep, fall asleep,
Suppose the man should fall asleep?
My fair Lady.

Give him a pipe to smoke all night,
Smoke all night, smoke all night,
Give him a pipe to smoke all night,
My fair Lady.

A DILLAR, A DOLLAR

In Yorkshire, 'diller' is used to describe a schoolboy who is dull and slow at learning. One scholar suggests that 'diller' and 'dollar' are shortened forms of dilatory and dullard, but just exactly what the words signify is not certain.

A dillar, a dollar,
A ten o'clock scholar,
What makes you come so soon?
You used to come at ten o'clock,
But now you come at noon.

COCK-A-DOODLE-DOO!

This very popular rhyme is associated with a somewhat gruesome event in Hertfordshire at the end of Elizabeth I's reign. The story, related in a pamphlet published in 1606, tells of the murder of a three-year-old boy, a deed witnessed by his slightly older sister, whose tongue was then cut out to prevent her naming the murderers. Some years later when she was playing with friends, the children began to 'mock the cock', a common game at that time, with the words, 'Cock a doodle dooe, Peggy hath lost her shoe'. Urged by a friend to repeat the words, the dumb girl miraculously opened her mouth and uttered the rhyme. The earliest printed version of the first four lines of the rhyme appeared in about 1765. The three other verses are probably of 19th century origin.

Cock-a-doodle-doo!
My dame has lost her shoe,
My master's lost his fiddling stick,
And doesn't know what to do.

Cock-a-doodle-doo!
What is my dame to do?
Till master finds his fiddling stick,
She'll dance without her shoe.

Cock-a-doodle-doo!
My dame has found her shoe,
And master's found his fiddling stick,
Sing cock-a-doodle-doo.

Cock-a-doodle-doo!
My dame will dance with you,
While master fiddles his fiddling stick,
For dame and doodle doo.

LITTLE TOMMY TUCKER

Tom Tucker is an ancient English and Scottish appellation for one who is voracious, takes everything, particularly at the expense of others. 'To sing for one's supper' has long been a commonplace phrase and was probably first used for the wandering troubadours of medieval times, who literally did just that in the inns and taverns of England.

Little Tommy Tucker
Sings for his supper;
What shall we give him?
White bread and butter.
How shall he cut it,
Without e'er a knife?
How shall he marry
Without e'er a wife?

Little Tommy Tucker,
Sing for your supper.
What shall he eat?
White bread and butter.

CHARLEY, CHARLEY

This rhyme is of relatively recent origin, dating from the late 19th century.

Charley, Charley, stole the barley,
Out of the baker's shop.
The baker came out and gave him a clout,
Which made poor Charley hop.

TWO LITTLE DICKY BIRDS

The earlier 18th century version
of this rhyme has 'Two little
blackbirds sitting on a
hill, / One named Jack and one
named Jill'. The names were
probably changed to those of the
Apostles in the 19th century.
The game which these verses
accompany is a simple
sleight-of-hand trick.

Two little dicky birds sitting on a wall;
One named Peter, one named Paul.
Fly away, Peter! Fly away Paul!
Come back, Peter! Come back, Paul!

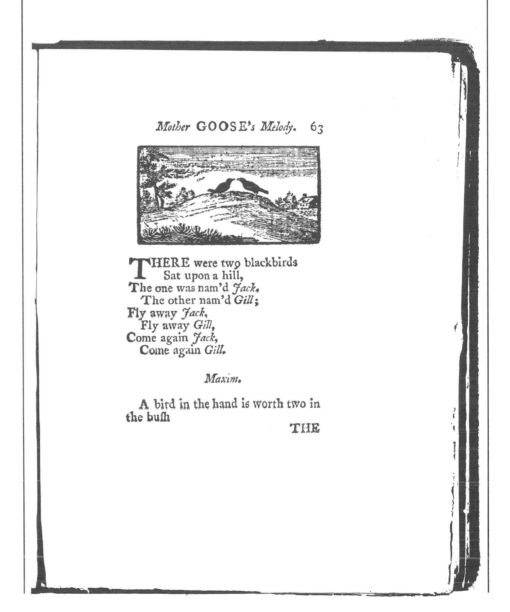

Mother GOOSE's *Melody.* 63

THERE were two blackbirds
   Sat upon a hill,
The one was nam'd *Jack,*
   The other nam'd *Gill;*
Fly away *Jack,*
   Fly away *Gill,*
Come again *Jack,*
   Come again *Gill.*

Maxim.

A bird in the hand is worth two in
the buſh
            THE

SIMPLE SIMON

The tale of Simple Simon may date from Elizabethan times and the *Oxford English Dictionary* confirms that, in the 18th century at least, Simple Simon meant 'a natural, a silly fellow'.

Simple Simon met a pieman,
Going to the fair;
Says Simple Simon to the pieman,
Let me taste your ware.

Says the pieman to Simple Simon,
Show me first your penny;
Says Simple Simon to the pieman,
Indeed I have not any.

Simple Simon went a-fishing
For to catch a whale;
All the water he had got
Was in his mother's pail.

SIMPLE SIMON MET A PIE-MAN

GOING · TO · THE · FAIR

BYAM SHAW

I HAD A LITTLE PONY

This version is first recorded in 1825, although an earlier one: 'I had a little bonny nag / His name was Dapple Grey; / And he would bring me to an ale-house, / A mile out of his way', seems to have been in existence since 1630.

I had a little pony,
His name was Dapple Grey;
I lent him to a lady
To ride a mile away.
She whipped him, she slashed him,
She rode him through the mire;
I would not lend my pony now,
For all the lady's hire.

MONDAY'S CHILD

There are numerous versions of
this well-known prophecy, all
dating from the 19th century.

Monday's child is fair of face,
Tuesday's child is full of grace,
Wednesday's child is full of woe,
Thursday's child has far to go,
Friday's child is loving and giving,
Saturday's child works hard for his living,
But the child that is born on the Sabbath day
Is bonny and blithe, and good and gay.

93

PUSSY CAT, PUSSY CAT, WHERE HAVE YOU BEEN?

It is widely thought that the queen here is Elizabeth I and that the rhyme refers to an actual incident that took place in her reign.

Pussy cat, pussy cat, where have you been?
I've been to London to see the Queen.
Pussy cat, pussy cat, what did you there?
I frightened a little mouse under her chair.

HERE WE GO ROUND THE MULBERRY BUSH

This dance game was particularly popular at the end of the 19th century. An earlier version mentions a bramble bush and another begins: 'Who will you have for nuts and May'.

Here we go round the mulberry bush,
The mulberry bush, the mulberry bush,
Here we go round the mulberry bush,
On a cold and frosty morning.

This is the way we clap our hands,
Clap our hands, clap our hands,
This is the way we clap our hands,
On a cold and frosty morning.

TWEEDLE-DUM AND TWEEDLE-DEE

We are perhaps most familiar with these twins from Alice's adventures *Through the Looking Glass*. However, in the 1720s, the composer Handel and an Italian musician, Giovanni Battista Bononcini, were enmeshed in a bitter rivalry. The public dispute was described by John Byrom, their contemporary and a writer of hymns, as follows: 'Some say, compared to Bononcini / That Mynheer Handel's but a ninny; / Others aver that he to Handel / Is scarcely fit to hold a candle; / Strange all this difference should be / Twixt tweedle-dum and tweedle-dee'. Whether Byrom was referring to an older rhyme or whether this rhyme is based on his doggerel we do not know.

Tweedle-dum and Tweedle-dee
Resolved to have a battle,
For Tweedle-dum said Tweedle-dee
Had spoiled his nice new rattle.
Just then flew by a monstrous crow,
As big as a tar-barrel,
Which frightened both the heroes so,
They quite forgot their quarrel.

WHAT ARE LITTLE BOYS MADE OF?

These verses have been attributed to the poet, Robert Southey, but there is little evidence to support this. The rhyme was a popular one from the mid-19th century onwards.

What are little boys made of?
What are little boys made of?
Frogs and snails,
And puppy-dogs' tails,
That's what little boys are made of.

What are little girls made of?
What are little girls made of?
Sugar and spice,
And all things nice,
That's what little girls are made of.

WHERE ARE YOU GOING TO, MY PRETTY MAID?

This appears to be a version, carefully rewritten for the nursery, of an old folksong dating from Tudor times about a milkmaid and a gentleman with dishonourable intentions. In times past, to ask a girl, in some country districts in England, if one might go milking with her amounted, almost, to a proposal of marriage.

Where are you going to, my pretty maid?
I'm going a-milking, sir, she said.

May I go with you, my pretty maid?
You're kindly welcome, sir, she said.

Say, will you marry me, my pretty maid?
Yes, if you please, kind sir, she said.

What is your father, my pretty maid?
My father's a farmer, sir, she said.

What is your fortune, my pretty maid?
My face is my fortune, sir, she said.

Then I can't marry you, my pretty maid.
Nobody asked you, sir, she said.

This jolly song has been known since the early 19th century at least. It is popular on both sides of the Atlantic and was a particular favourite with 19th century nursery rhyme illustrators.

A fox jumped up one winter's night,
And begged the moon to give him light,
For he'd many miles to trot that night
Before he reached his den O!
Den O! den O!
For he'd many miles to trot that night
Before he reached his den O!

The first place he came to was a farmer's yard,
Where the ducks and the geese declared it hard
That their nerves should be shaken and their rest so
    marred
By a visit from Mr Fox O!
Fox O! Fox O!
That their nerves should be shaken and their rest so
    marred
By a visit from Mr Fox O!

He took the grey goose by the neck
And swung him right across his back;
The grey goose cried out Quack, quack, quack,
With his legs hanging dangling down O!
Down O! down O!
The grey goose cried out Quack, quack, quack,
With his legs hanging dangling down O!

Old Mother Slipper Slopper jumped out of bed,
And out of the window she popped her head;
Oh! John, John, John, the grey goose is gone,
And the fox is off to his den O!
Den O! den O!
Oh! John, John, John, the grey goose is gone,
And the fox is off to his den O!

John ran up to the top of the hill,
And blew his whistle loud and shrill;
Said the fox, That is very pretty music; still –
I'd rather be in my den O!
Den O! den O!
Said the fox, That is very pretty music; still –
I'd rather be in my den O!

The fox went back to his hungry den,
And his dear little foxes, eight, nine, ten;
Quoth they, Good daddy, you must go there again,
If you bring such good cheer from the farm O!
Farm O! farm O!
Quoth they, Good daddy, you must go there again,
If you bring such good cheer from the farm O!

The fox and his wife, without any strife,
Said they never ate a better goose in all their life;
They did very well without fork or knife,
And the little ones picked the bones O!
Bones O! bones O!
They did very well without fork or knife,
And the little ones picked the bones O!

LITTLE POLLY FLINDERS

The first line of this rhyme, published in 1805, has 'Little Jenny Flinders'. This later version was particularly popular in the late 19th century.

Little Polly Flinders
Sat among the cinders,
Warming her pretty little toes.
Her mother came and caught her,
And whipped her little daughter
For spoiling her nice new clothes.

DIDDLE, DIDDLE, DUMPLING, MY SON JOHN

'Diddle, diddle, dumpling' was the cry of the hot dumpling sellers in the streets of London. One authority states that 'it might be surmised that John went to bed fuddled, and not from eating dumplings'. The rhyme was a favourite of Charles Lamb, who included a Latin version of it in one of his letters.

Diddle, diddle, dumpling, my son John,
Went to bed with his trousers on;
One shoe off, one shoe on,
Diddle, diddle, dumpling, my son John.

IF ALL THE WORLD WERE PAPER

This rhyme was well-known in the reign of Charles I. It is possible that it is a parody of the extravagant language used in ancient Jewish and medieval ecclesiastical rituals. An ode sung in synagogues during the first day of Pentecost begins: 'Could we with ink the ocean fill. . . / And were the skies of parchment made. . .' The Koran contains passages using the same imagery and there are many parallels in the folksongs of Germany, Serbia, Albania, Italy and Greece.

If all the world were paper,
And all the sea were ink,
If all the trees were bread and cheese,
What would we have to drink?

RAIN, RAIN, GO AWAY

John Aubrey noted in 1687 that this charm, sung by children, is of great antiquity and indeed, a version of it was known in ancient Greece. Children all over the world still chant it, although there are local variations. In England, 'Rain, rain go to Spain / Never show your face again.' is an alternative version.

Rain, rain, go away,
Come again another day.

THERE WAS AN OLD WOMAN WHO LIVED IN A SHOE

This rhyme, a version of which first appeared in print in 1797, is probably very old and may have some folklore significance. Casting a shoe after the bride when she goes on her honeymoon is an ancient custom, associated with the fertility of the union. This is consistent with the many children the lady who lived in the shoe had.

There was an old woman who lived in a shoe,
She had so many children she didn't know what to
    do.
She gave them some broth without any bread;
She whipped them all soundly and put them to bed.

TO MARKET, TO MARKET

A version of this knee-trotting rhyme has been known since the early 17th century, although this well-known version is comparatively modern.

To market, to market, to buy a fat pig,
Home again, home again, jiggety jig.
To market, to market, to buy a fat hog,
Home again, home again, jiggety jog.

HICKETY PICKETY, MY BLACK HEN

This is probably a cleaner version of an older rhyme about Little Blue Betty, a lady of easy virtue.

Hickety Pickety, my black hen,
She lay eggs for gentlemen;
Sometimes nine, and sometimes ten,
Hickety Pickety, my black hen.

TO MARKET - 1 MILE

RING-A-RING O'ROSES

This rhyme, the accompaniment of one of the most popular of nursery ring games, first appeared in print surprisingly late in Kate Greenaway's *Mother Goose* (1881). It is widely believed that it is associated with the Great Plague, the 'roses' referring to the rosy rash which was one of the symptoms of the plague, the 'posies', the herbs and spices carried as a protection against the infection (and still carried ritually – as an antidote to gaol fever – by Old Bailey judges at the opening of each session) and the sneezing a final, fatal symptom before falling down dead. The editors of the *Oxford Dictionary of Nursery Rhymes* are dismissive of this interpretation, but the belief is so widely and so strongly held that, even if unfounded, it is now a popular myth.

Ring-a-ring o'roses,
A pocket full of posies,
A-tishoo! A-tishoo!
We all fall down.

Flight of the townspeople to the country to escape the plague, 1630

110

Ring-a-ring-a-roses,
A pocket full of posies;
Hush! hush! hush! hush!
We're all tumbled down.

THE QUEEN OF HEARTS

One of the best-known of nursery rhymes, this was a favourite with children in the late 18th century and was used by Charles Lamb in 1805 for a nursery rhyme book. Its present fame may well be attributed to its use by Lewis Carroll in *Alice in Wonderland*.

The Queen of Hearts
She made some tarts,
All on a summer's day;
The Knave of Hearts
He stole the tarts,
And took them clean away.

And took them quite away

How like a thievish Jack he looks!
I wish for my part all the cooks
Would come and baste him with a ladle
As long as ever they were able.
To keep his fingers ends from itching
After sweet things in the Queen's kitchen.

The King of Hearts
Called for the tarts,
And beat the Knave full sore;
The Knave of Hearts
Brought back the tarts,
And vowed he'd steal no more.

Rub-a-dub-dub!
Three men in a tub,
And who do you
   think they be?
The butcher, the baker,
The candlestick-maker,
Run 'em down,
   knaves all three!

RUB-A-DUB-DUB

An early version of this rhyme
mentions three maids in the tub
(presumably unclothed), a side
show attraction at a local fair
which these respectable
tradesmen no doubt stealthily
enjoyed.

Rub-a-dub-dub,
Three men in a tub;
And who do you think they be?
The butcher, the baker,
The candlestick-maker;
They all jumped out of a rotten potato,
Turn'em out, knaves all three!

117

SING A SONG OF SIXPENCE

This rhyme can be traced back to the 16th century, although much nonsense has been written about its origins, not least of which is that it refers to, respectively, the 24 hours of the day; to Henry VIII, Catherine of Aragon and Anne Boleyn; and the printing of the English Bible. It would seem, however, that some 16th century cookbooks actually did contain recipes for baking pies using live birds which, when the pie was cut, would fly out creating a spectacular, if somewhat alarming, diversion at a banquet. The 'pocketful of rye' may well have been a common form of measurement, and the 'counting house' (referred to on several occasions in *The Merry Wives of Windsor*) was the office where an establishment's business was conducted.

Sing a song of sixpence,
A pocket full of rye;
Four and twenty blackbirds
Baked in a pie.

When the pie was opened
The birds began to sing;
Was not that a dainty dish
To set before the king?

The king was in his counting house
Counting out his money;
The queen was in the parlour
Eating bread and honey.

The maid was in the garden
Hanging out the clothes;
There came a little blackbird,
And snapped off her nose.

TOM, TOM, THE PIPER'S SON

Tom's pig was not a live one but a sweetmeat, sold by street hawkers particularly in the 18th century. This rhyme is often confused with: 'Tom, he was a piper's son / He learnt to play when he was young / And all the tune that he could play / Was "over the hills and far away"', as Pigling Bland did in Beatrix Potter's story.

Late 18th century engraving of a pig pie man

Tom, Tom, the piper's son,
Stole a pig and away did run;
The pig was eat, and Tom was beat,
And Tom went crying down the street.

I SAW THREE SHIPS COME SAILING BY

Versions of this rhyme have been known since the early 19th century, and later it was a popular subject for nursery rhyme illustrators.

I saw three ships come sailing by,
Come sailing by, come sailing by,
I saw three ships come sailing by,
On New Year's Day in the morning.

And what do you think was in them then,
Was in them then, was in them then?
And what do you think was in them then
On New Year's Day in the morning?

Three pretty girls were in them then,
Were in them then, were in them then,
Three pretty girls were in them then,
On New Year's Day in the morning.

One could whistle, and one could sing,
And one could play on the violin,
Such joy there was at my wedding,
On New Year's Day in the morning.

YANKEE DOODLE

'Yankee' is a word of doubtful origin. According to an officer in General Burgoyne's army it was derived from a Cherokee word meaning coward or slave and 'was bestowed upon the residents of New England by Virginians for not assisting them in a war with the Cherokees'. Certainly the song was sung with derision by the British troops at the outbreak of the War of Independence, but after the battle of Bunker Hill, it was taken up by the Americans as a battle cry. The 'macaroni' here refers to something that might be worn by a fop (a macaroni).

18th century print of attack on Bunker Hill and burning of Charleston

Yankee Doodle went to town,
Riding on a pony;
He stuck a feather in his cap
And called it macaroni.

A WISE OLD OWL

Although this is said to be old, it is not known before World War I. Calvin Coolidge is said to have had the words inscribed over the fireplace in his house.

A wise old owl lived in an oak;
The more he saw the less he spoke.
The less he spoke the more he heard.
Why can't we all be like that wise old bird?

MARY, MARY, QUITE CONTRARY

Some versions of this rhyme begin 'Mistress Mary' and it is widely supposed to refer to Mary, Queen of Scots, whose frivolous French ways and Roman Catholic upbringing were disapproved of by John Knox (it was she who, with her cousin, Elizabeth I, formed Knox's famous 'monstrous regiment of women'). The pretty maids were possibly her ladies-in-waiting, the 'four Marys' (Mary Beaton, Mary Seaton, Mary Fleming and Mary Livingston) and it has been further suggested that the cockleshells were the decorations on a gown given to her by the Dauphin.

Mary, Queen of Scots, reproved by John Knox. Painting by W. Frith

126

Mary, Mary, quite contrary,
How does your garden grow?
With silver bells and cockle shells,
And pretty maids all in a row.

PAT A CAKE

This was known as early as 1698
and often accompanies a hand
clapping or hand warming game.

Pat a cake, pat a cake, baker's man,
Bake me a cake as fast as you can.
Pat it and prick it, and mark it with T,
And put it in the oven for Tommy and me.

THE LION AND THE UNICORN

Popular tradition states that this tells the story of the union of Scotland (whose royal coat of arms bore two unicorns) and England when James VI of Scotland became James I of England in 1603. Lewis Carroll refers to it in *Through the Looking Glass* as the words of an old song which presumably it was, with many verses now lost.

The Lion and the Unicorn were fighting for the
    crown;
The Lion beat the Unicorn all round about the town.

Some gave them white bread, some gave them
    brown;
Some gave them plum cake, and drummed them out
    of town.

PLEASE TO REMEMBER

The fifth of November is, of course, still remembered in England as Guy Fawkes' Day when bonfires are lit around the 'Guy', a stuffed figure which children take about the streets for a week or so preceding November 5th, begging for fireworks money ('a penny for the Guy'). The Gunpowder Plot of 1605 led by the ardent Roman Catholic, Guy Fawkes, was almost successful. He and his fellow-conspirators, who planned to blow up the Houses of Parliament and so rid the country of its Protestant rulers, had, in fact, planted the gunpowder and set the fuses, having dug their way to beneath the House of Lords from an adjoining house. Someone, however, warned a friend to keep away from the House on the set day, November 6th. A search was made and on the night of November 4th, the plot was discovered.

Please to remember
The Fifth of November,
Gunpowder, treason and plot;
I see no reason why gunpowder treason
Should ever be forgot.

Bates.   R. Winter.   C. Wright.   J. Wright.   Percy.   Fawkes.   Catesby.   T. Winter.

Contemporary print of Guy Fawkes and his conspirators

THIS IS THE HOUSE THAT JACK BUILT

This accumulative rhyme first appeared in print in 1755 but is probably very old and may well be derived from a Hebrew chant known in the 16th century. Similar rhymes occur in other European languages.

This is the house that Jack built.

This is the malt
That lay in the house that Jack built.

This is the rat
That ate the malt
That lay in the house that Jack built.

This is the cat
That killed the rat,
That ate the malt
That lay in the house that Jack built.

This is the dog,
That worried the cat,
That killed the rat,
That ate the malt
That lay in the house that Jack built.

131

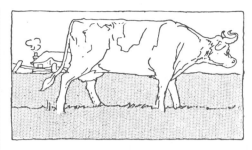

This is the cow with the crumpled horn,
That tossed the dog,
That worried the cat,
That killed the rat,
That ate the malt
That lay in the house that Jack built.

This is the maiden all forlorn,
That milked the cow with the crumpled horn,
That tossed the dog,
That worried the cat,
That killed the rat,
That ate the malt
That lay in the house that Jack built.

This is the man all tattered and torn,
That kissed the maiden all forlorn,
That milked the cow with the crumpled horn,
That tossed the dog,
That worried the cat,
That killed the rat,
That ate the malt
That lay in the house that Jack built.

This is the priest all shaven and shorn,
That married the man all tattered and torn,
That kissed the maiden all forlorn,
That milked the cow with the crumpled horn,
That tossed the dog,
That worried the cat,
That killed the rat,
That ate the malt
That lay in the house that Jack built.

This is the cock that crowed in the morn,
That waked the priest all shaven and shorn,
That married the man all tattered and torn,
That kissed the maiden all forlorn,
That milked thc cow with the crumpled horn,
That tossed the dog,
That worried the cat,
That killed the rat,
That ate the malt
That lay in the house that Jack built.

This is the farmer sowing his corn,
That kept the cock that crowed in the morn,
That waked the priest all shaven and shorn,
That married the man all tattered and torn,
That kissed the maiden all forlorn,
That milked the cow with the crumpled horn,
That tossed the dog,
That worried the cat,
That killed the rat,
That ate the malt
That lay in the house that Jack built.

LUCY LOCKET

This Kitty Fisher is probably the famous 18th century courtesan and some-time actress. She was a friend and neighbour of Dr Johnson's and achieved notoriety as the mistress of a number of eminent men. By the middle of the 19th century the rhyme was well known in both England and America and was sung to the tune of 'Yankee Doodle'.

Kitty Fisher (d. 1767)

Lucy Locket lost her pocket,
Kitty Fisher found it;
There was not a penny in it,
Only ribbon round it.

134

Little Jack Horner sat in a corner,
Eating a Christmas pie :   plum,
he put in his thumb, and pull'd out a
And said 'What a good boy am I !'

LITTLE JACK HORNER

The legend surrounding this rhyme is that the original Jack Horner was the steward to Richard Whiting, abbot of Glastonbury in Somerset, the richest abbey in the kingdom at the time of Henry VIII. At the time of the Dissolution of the Monasteries the abbot, hoping to gain favour with the king, sent his steward to London with a Christmas gift. This was a pie, in which were contained the title deeds of twelve manors, one of which Jack Horner extracted on his journey. In fact, soon after the Dissolution, the manor of Mells became the residence of Thomas Horner, and his descendants still live there. In Tudor times, as now, anybody could be called Jack, particularly if he was thought to be a knave; and Thomas Horner was a member of the jury that condemned Abbot Whiting to death. A rhyme still current in Somerset and first recorded in 1860 runs: 'Hopton, Horner, Smyth and Thynne. / When the abbots went out, they came in.' Sir John Thynne, incidentally, built Longleat House, one of the finest examples of Elizabethan architecture in England. It is on record, also, that in the relevant period Abbot Whiting sent several Christmas gifts to the king.

Little Jack Horner,
Sat in a corner,
Eating a Christmas pie.
He put in his thumb,
And pulled out a plum,
And said What a good boy am I.

135

SOLOMON GRUNDY

This rhyme was probably devised to teach children the names of the days of the week and has remained popular since it was first recorded in the 19th century.

Solomon Grundy,
Born on Monday,
Christened on Tuesday,
Married on Wednesday,
Took ill on Thursday,
Worse on Friday,
Died on Saturday,
Buried on Sunday,
This is the end
Of Solomon Grundy.

PETER PIPER

This tongue twister which first appeared in print in 1815, has been recommended as a cure for hiccups if it is said three times in one breath.

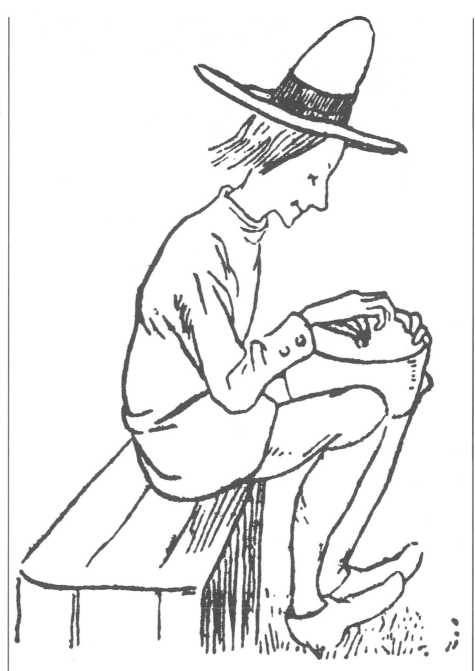

Peter Piper picked a peck of pickled pepper;
A peck of pickled pepper Peter Piper picked;
If Peter Piper picked a peck of pickled pepper,
Where's the peck of pickled pepper Peter Piper
        picked?

Little Miss Muffet,
She sat on a tuffet,
Eating of curds and whey;
There came a great spider,
Who sat down beside her,
And frighten'd Miss Muffet
away.

LITTLE MISS MUFFET

Of all nursery rhymes this verse appears most frequently in children's books. It has been suggested that Miss Muffet was Patience, the daughter of a 16th century entomologist, Dr Thomas Muffet, the author of a work in verse entitled *The Silkworms and their flies*, and a man 'whose admiration for spiders has never been surpassed'. Since no record of the rhyme has been found earlier than 1805, this is a speculative but interesting theory. Miss Muffet probably sat on a grassy mound, though 'tuffet' can also mean a three-legged stool. The 'curds and whey' which Miss Muffet was eating is a form of junket, the curds the thick part of the milk, the whey, the watery part.

Little Miss Muffet,
Sat on a tuffet,
Eating her curds and whey.
Along came a spider,
Who sat down beside her,
And frightened Miss Muffet away.

I LOVE LITTLE PUSSY

This first appeared in print in 1830 and was thereafter included in a number of nursery rhyme books throughout the 19th century.

I love little pussy, her coat is so warm,
And if I don't hurt her she'll do me no harm.
So I'll not pull her tail, nor drive her away,
But pussy and I very gently will play.

EARLY TO BED, EARLY TO RISE

In 19th century nursery rhyme books this proverb (known from at least the 15th century) is often preceded by another old proverb: 'The cock crows in the morn / To tell us to rise, / And he that lies late / Will never be wise'. The rhyme has been much parodied. James Thurber's witty version is: 'Early to rise and early to bed makes a man healthy, wealthy and dead.'

Early to bed and early to rise
Makes a man healthy, wealthy, and wise.

142

JACK AND JILL

In *Mother Goose's Melody* (1765) a woodcut illustration to this rhyme shows two boys, which has led at least one commentator to identify the two as Cardinal Wolsey and his coadjutor, Bishop Tarbes, who together went to France to arrange the marriage of Mary Tudor to the French monarch. Another asserts that it is of great antiquity, with its origins in Scandinavian mythology, while Lewis Spence in *Myth and Ritual* (1947) maintains that some ancient mystic ceremony may be associated with the rhyme since 'no one in a folklore sense climbs to the top of a hill for water unless that water has special significance.' But, as the editors of the *Oxford Dictionary of Nursery Rhymes* have pointed out, the fact that 'after' rhymes with 'water' suggests that the rhyme may have originated in the 17th century.

Jack and Jill went up the hill
To fetch a pail of water;
Jack fell down and broke his crown
And Jill came tumbling after.

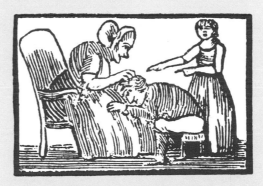

Up Jack got and home did trot
As fast as he could caper;
Went to bed and bound his head
With vinegar and brown paper.

When Jill came in how she did grin
To see Jack's paper plaster;
Mother vexed, did whip her next
For causing Jack's disaster.

I'LL TELL YOU A STORY

'Jack a Nory' goes by other names in different versions of this rhyme, used to discourage children's demands for a story.

I'll tell you a story
About Jack-a-Nory,
And now my story's begun;
I'll tell you another
About Jack and his brother,
And now my story is done.

THE MAN IN
THE MOON

According to legend, the moon has been inhabited for centuries by a man with a bundle of sticks on his back, who was banished there for gathering sticks on the Sabbath. The rhyme was certainly popular in the 19th century and is mentioned by Mrs Micawber in *David Copperfield*, although it probably dates from at least a century earlier when plum porridge had not yet been cemented into plum pudding by the use of a pudding cloth.

The man in the moon
Came tumbling down,
And asked his way to Norwich;
He went by the south,
And burnt his mouth
With supping cold plum porridge.

THE LADY OF THE LAKE TELLETH ARTHVR OF THE SWORD EXCALIBVR

When good King Arthur ruled this land,
He was a goodly king;
He stole three pecks of barley-meal,
To make a bag-pudding.

Arthur appears as 'King Stephen' in other versions of this ancient song or ballad, which may well have been introduced into an old play possibly in the 16th or 17th century.

A bag-pudding the king did make,
And stuffed it well with plums;
And in it put great lumps of fat,
As big as my two thumbs.

The king and queen did eat thereof,
And noblemen beside;
And what they could not eat that night,
The queen next morning fried.

CLAP HANDS, CLAP HANDS

This game for infant amusement has many versions. All involve taking the child's hands, clapping them and repeating the little rhyme which always begins 'clap hands'.

Clap hands, clap hands,
Till father comes home;
For father's got money,
But mother's got none.

THREE LITTLE KITTENS THEY LOST THEIR MITTENS

These verses were first printed in *New Nursery Songs for All Good Children* (1853) and are often attributed to the book's author, Eliza Follen, a New Englander. She, however, describes them as 'traditional'.

Three little kittens they lost their mittens,
And they began to cry,
Oh, mother dear, we sadly fear
That we have lost our mittens.
What! lost your mittens, you naughty kittens!
Then you shall have no pie.
Mee-ow, mee-ow, mee-ow.
No, you shall have no pie.

The three little kittens they found their mittens,
And they began to cry,
Oh, mother dear, see here, see here,
For we have found our mittens.
Put on your mittens, you silly kittens,
And you may have some pie.
Purr-r, purr-r, purr-r,
Oh, let us have some pie.

The three little kittens put on their mittens,
And soon ate up the pie;
Oh, mother dear, we greatly fear
That we have soiled our mittens.
What! soiled your mittens, you naughty kittens!
Then they began to sigh.
Mee-ow, mee-ow, mee-ow.
Then they began to sigh.

The three little kittens they washed their mittens,
And hung them out to dry;
Oh, mother dear, do not you hear
That we have washed our mittens?
What! washed your mittens! then you're good
    kittens,
But I smell a rat close by.
Mee-ow, mee-ow, mee-ow.
We smell a rat close by.

151

OLD MOTHER GOOSE

This story of the goose that laid the golden egg was first recorded in about 1815.

Old Mother Goose, when
She wanted to wander,
Would ride through the air
On a very find gander.

Mother Goose had a house,
'Twas built in a wood,
Where an owl at the door
For a sentinel stood.

She had a son Jack,
A plain-looking lad,
He was not very good
Nor yet very bad.

She sent him to market
A live goose he bought,
Here, mother, says he,
It will not go for nought.

Jack's goose and her gander
Grew very fond;
They'd both eat together
Or swim in one pond.

Jack found one morning,
As I have been told,
His goose had laid him
An egg of pure gold.

Jack rode to his mother
The news for to tell;
She called him a good boy
And said it was well.

Jack sold his gold egg
To a merchant untrue
Who cheated him out of
The half of his due.

Then Jack went a-courting
A lady so gay,
As fair as the lily
And sweet as the May.

The merchant and the squire
Soon came at his back,
And began to belabour
The sides of poor Jack.

But old Mother Goose
That instant came in,
And turned her son Jack
Into famed Harlequin.

She then with her wand
Touched the lady so fine
And turned her at once
Into sweet Columbine.

The gold egg in the sea
Was thrown away then –
When Jack jumped in
And got it again.

And Old Mother Goose
The goose saddled soon
And mounting its back
Flew up to the moon.

LAVENDER'S BLUE

A printed version of this old ballad first appeared in the late 17th century. Perhaps the most familiar version nowadays is that of the song, *Lavender Blue*, recorded for Walt Disney's film of 1948, *So Dear to My Heart*, and sung by Dinah Shore, which became an immediate 'hit' on both sides of the Atlantic.

Lavender's blue, dilly, dilly, lavender's green,
When I am king, dilly, dilly, you shall be queen;
Call up your men, dilly, dilly, set them to work,
Some to the plough, dilly, dilly, some to the cart;
Some to make hay, dilly, dilly, some to thresh corn;
Whilst you and I, dilly, dilly, keep ourselves warm.

OH WHERE, OH WHERE HAS MY LITTLE DOG GONE?

Written by a Philadelphian music publisher and critic, Septimus Winner, the original version of this song, *Der Deitcher's Dog*, was published in 1864 as a comic ballad. Although now forgotten, its nursery version is still popular throughout the English-speaking world.

Oh where, oh where has my little dog gone?
Oh where, oh where can he be?
With his ears cut short and his tail cut long,
Oh where, oh where is he?

I DO NOT LIKE THEE, DOCTOR FELL

The Dr Fell (1625-86) referred to here was the Dean of Christ Church, Oxford. The rhyme first appears in the works of the satirist, Thomas Brown, who, it is said, was threatened with expulsion from Oxford unless he could translate, on the spot, the lines of Roman poet Martial, 'Non amo te, Sabidi, nec possum dicere quare; Hoc tantum possum dicere, Non amo te'. Brown's translation was this verse.

Below right: 19th century engraving of Christ Church, Oxford
Dr John Fell (1625-86)

I do not like thee, Doctor Fell,
The reason why I cannot tell;
But this I know, and know full well,
I do not like thee, Doctor Fell.

INDEX of first lines

ACKNOWLEDGEMENTS

The sources for the pictures in this book are shown below. The editor would like to extend special thanks to Miss Irene Whalley and the staff of the Library, Victoria and Albert Museum, London and to Paul Dinnage; in addition, to J. M. Dent & Sons Ltd, William Heinemann Ltd and Frederick Warne Ltd. If the publishers have unwittingly infringed copyright in any illustration reproduced they will gladly pay an appropriate fee on being satisfied as to the owner's title.

The black and white illustrations on pages **25, 27, 32** (lower), **36** (lower right), **44** (lower), **52** (all except the third picture), **53, 81, 89** (upper), **92** (lower), **96** (upper), **124** (upper), **128** (lower), **135, 143, 144** (lower), **153,** and **154,** come from *The Oxford Nursery Rhyme Book,* Copyright Iona and Peter Opie, Published by the Oxford University Press. The illustration on **p.120** (lower left) comes from *The Oxford Dictionary of Nursery Rhymes,* Copyright Iona and Peter Opie, Published by the Oxford University Press.

Beardsley, A. *Le Morte d'Arthur,* 1893. **146:** Bedford, F. D. *Original Poems and Others,* 1904. **2:** Bewick, T. *The Figures of Bewick's Quadrapeds, 1824.* **140, 141, 156:** Bewick, T. *A History of British Birds,* Vol. I. 1797. **125:** Bewick, T. & J. *Select Fables,* 1820. **144:** The British Library, London. **147:** Brooke, L. L. *Nursery Rhymes, Songs and Ditties,* 1916. **5, 92, 122:** Brooke, L. L. *Ring-a-Ring o'Roses,* 1976. **36, 44, 48, 57, 73, 85, 108, 109, 110, 129, 145:** Caldecott, R. *Picture Book No 2,* 1880. **114, 115, 118:** Carroll, L. *Through the Looking Glass,* 1872. **96:** *A Child's Gift,* c1835. **81:** *Cock Robin and the New Mother Hubbard,* c1850, **35, 51:** Comus, *Mr Fox,* 1857. **99:** Comus, *Three Kittens,* 1859. **151:** Courtauld Institute of Art, London, **60:** *Cradle Melodies,* c1835. **135:** Crane, W. *Baby's Opera,* 1877. **31, 38, 39, 47, 54, 55, 95, 123, 127, 142, 147:** Crane, W. *New Toy Book,* 1873. **70, 71, 75:** *Denslow's Mother goose,* 1902. **19, 74, 103:** *The Diverting History of Old Mother Hubbard and her Dog* c1815. **53:** *Favourite Rhymes for the Nursery,* 1907. **105:** Folkard, C. *The Land of Nursery Rhyme,* 1932. **20, 37, 48, 58, 72, 97, 102, 136, 156:** Fraser, C. L. *Nursery rhymes,* 1919. **29, 120:** Greenaway, K. *April Baby's Book of Tunes,* 1900. **11, 94, 98, 102, 108, 139:** Greenaway, K. *Mother Goose,* 1881. **18, 30, 42, 111, 126, 134:** *The History of an Apple Pie,* c1810. **25:** Hugo, T. *Bewick's Woodcuts,* 1870. **22, 77:** Lamb, C. *The King and Queen of Hearts,* 1809. **113:** Le Mair, H. W. *Little Songs of Long Ago,* 1912. **62, 63, 78, 83, 155:** Leaden Press, *1000 Quaint Cuts,* n.d. **52:** *Little Rhymes for Little Folk,* c1823, **7:** Loomis, C. *Familiar Rhymes of Mother Goose,* 1888. **11, 27, 58, 67, 90, 107, 116:** Lucas, E. V. *The Book of Shops,* 1899. **43, 130:** Millais, J. E. *Little Songs for Me to Sing,* 1865. **72:** *Mother Goose's Melody,* 1791. **9, 28, 36, 56, 89:** *Mother Goose's Nursery Rhymes and Fairy Tales,* 1892. **12, 24, 25, 50, 84, 96, 125, 140, 152:** *National Nursery Rhymes and Songs,* 1870. **140:** National Portrait Gallery, London. **10, 18, 23, 33, 72, 73, 134:** *Nurse Dandlem's Little Repository,* c1820. **92:** *Nursery Rhymes* c1830. **27, 32, 144:** *Nursery Rhymes for Children,* c1840, **36:** *Nursery Rhymes with Coloured Pictures,* 1866. **106:** *Old Mother Goose, or the Golden Egg,* c1820. **153, 154:** *Old Mother Hubbard and her Dog,* c1840. **52:** Oxford University Press, **157:** Peake, M. *Ride a Cock-Horse,* 1940. **65, 117:** *Picture Book of the Nursery,* 1867. **10, 34:** *Pleasing Popular Nursery Rhymes,* 1858. **129:** Prado Museum, Madrid, **54:** Rackham, A. *Mother Goose Nursery Rhymes,* 1913. **14, 28, 38, 50, 56, 61, 64, 104, 120:** Rhys, E. & G. *Mother Goose's Book of Nursery Rhymes and Songs,* 1910. **28, 66, 137:** Robinson, C. *The Big Book of Nursery Rhymes,* 1911. **1, 9, 13, 16, 21, 23, 24, 26, 32, 40, 46, 49, 76, 80, 88, 93, 97, 100, 101, 112, 121, 131, 132, 133, 141, 148, 154, 157, 158, 160:** Rogers, J. E. *Ridicula Rediviva,* 1869. **67, 86, 87, 135, 138:** Shaw, B. *Old King Cole's Book of Nursery Rhymes,* 1901. **15, 45, 59, 91:** Sheffield City Art Gallery, **128:** *Tommy Thumb's Song Book,* 1788. **96:** Trusler, Rev J. *The Progress of Man and Society,* 1791. **77:** *Vocal Harmony, or No Song, No Supper,* c1800. **32, 44, 89, 92:** Wheeler, D. M. *Mother Goose's Nursery Rhymes,* 1928. **128:**